THE

RELIGION OF SCIENCE

BY

DR. PAUL CARUS

SECOND EDITION, REVISED AND ENLARGED

My people are destroyed for lack of knowledge.
Because thou hast rejected knowledge, I will also reject
thee that thou shalt be no priest to me. Hosea 4, 6.

Hold fast as a refuge to the truth. Buddha.

Watchmaker Publishing
1896

PREFACE.

THE work of The Open Court Publishing Company, appears
to be of purely theoretical importance ; but it pursues, nevertheless, an eminently practical aim, which, briefly expressed, is to
propound, develop, and establish the Religion of Science.

The present booklet aims to sketch the isagogics of the Religion of Science, intending to serve as an introduction to it, to prevent misconceptions, and to impart general information concerning
its principles and scope.

In order to establish the Religion of Science it is by no means
necessary to abolish the old religions, but only to purify them and
develop their higher possibilities, so that their mythologies shall be
changed into strictly scientific conceptions. It is intended to pre-
serve of the old religions all that is true and good, but to purify
their faith by rejecting superstitions and irrational elements, and
to discard, unrelentingly, their errors.

*   *   *

The churches of to-day still pursue a policy which closes their
doors to those who dare to think for themselves. Thus, the scientist and the philosopher will most likely shake their heads at the
idea of broadening the established religions and developing them into
the Religion of Science. which will stand upon scientifically provable truth, and will base our religious views upon that one and omnipresent revelation which is found in nature. But the undertaking
is not quite as hopeless as it appears. The churches, and especially
the American churches, are not as conservative and stationary as

their dogmas pretend to be. Almost all our churches have, during the last two decades, grown immensely in depth and catholicity. There is a very strong tendency among them to get rid of sectarian narrowness and dogmatic crudities. The influence of science is felt in our religious life everywhere, and its ultimate aim, although we are still very far from it, can but be a rationalising of the religious faith and a broadening of the sectarian creeds into one cosmical religion, which will be the only true and catholic faith, the religion of truth, i. e., of scientific truth, the Religion of Science.

*   *   *

We must introduce, on the one hand, the warmth of religious enthusiasm into the province of philosophy and science, and, on the other hand, the spirit of uncompromising criticism and scientific research into the domain of religious conviction.

We must learn to know that Science is but another name for Revelation.

*   *   *

The Religion of Science is an appeal to all mankind. It appeals to all lovers of truth within the churches and without.

Luther said somewhere, "The worst idols in the country are the sacraments and the altar"; and Luther's criticism is pertinent still. The Religion of Science comes to protest against the idolatry of our churches and against their pagan spirit which alone brings them into conflict with science.

*   *   *

The name, "Religion of Science," has not been invented to denote a schism, but to proclaim a principle which opposes not the faith of the churches, not their moral spirit, not their Christianity, but their dogmatism, their trust in rituals and their paganism.

The Religion of Science is not intended to be a new sect among the many other sects that now exist. The Religion of Science is no visible church with a definite number of members, having a constitution, by-laws, and a creed. The Religion of Science is the invisible church, and its members are all those who, like ourselves, believe in the religion of truth, who acknowledge that truth has not been revealed once and once only, but that we are constantly facing the revelation of truth, and that the scientific method of searching for truth is the same in religious matters as in other fields.

Those who profess the principles of the Religion of Science may belong to any church or to no church. They may, without becoming indifferent to distinctions, call themselves Christians, or Jews, or believers in the Religion of Humanity, or Freethinkers. Their bond of union is not a common ritual, nor forms, nor ceremonies, but the common aim of searching for, of trusting in, and of living in agreement with, the truth. And this hallowed community of the invisible church is no mere illusion.

To this invisible church belong Confucius, Zarathustra, Moses, Buddha, Christ, all the prophets, the saints, the investigators of truth, the inventors, the leaders of mankind, the learned and the great; and also all the humble, the meek, the poor in spirit, those who hunger for the spiritual gifts which the heroes of thought and deed have procured in their hard struggles for progress and for the realisation of human ideals.

*　　*　　*

The idea of the Religion of Science is as little Utopian as was the possibility of developing astronomy from astrology, or chemistry from alchemy, for the progress from the old dogmatic religions to the religion based upon our knowledge of the facts of nature is exactly of the same kind.

Religions develop naturally. The religions of to-day are not, as some of their adherents pretend, the product of a supernatural revelation, but are based upon the science of the times when they were founded. Our religion must embody the maturest, surest, and best established knowledge of to-day.

The Religion of Science is still a voice crying in the wilderness. Yet it comes from the heart of mankind and cannot be suppressed. Should it remain unheeded, it will be repeated by others that shall come after us, until its warning be heard and obeyed.

We do not hope to reach our aim in the near future, but we are confident that our ideal is sound, and that the eventual evolution of the religious views of mankind will justify our hopes.

TABLE OF CONTENTS.

INTRODUCTION.

INTRODUCTION.

We are born into the world as living, feeling, and thinking beings. We live for a while and then we die.

And what is our life? We toil, we suffer, we hope, we aspire, we work. Our joys are fleeting, and many of them leave behind them the lees of regret and disappointment. Only a few hopes are realised, only some aspirations are fulfilled, and only a part of our efforts is crowned with success.

Thus our life appears as a transient phenomenon, narrow in its field, short in its span of years, and limited in its power of achievement.

What shall be our aim and purpose?

Shall we look for satisfaction in the little gratifications that come from the pleasures of life? And is there no higher object than to live and be merry and pass away as though we had never been?

We anxiously look for support in tribulations, for comfort in afflictions, and for guidance in the vicissitudes of life. And the assistance that we find is our religion.

How can we acquire information concerning ourselves and the world in which we live? How shall we find a religion?

Information can be had only through inquiry. We have to prove all things and hold fast that which is good. Says Jesus of Nazareth: "Seek and ye shall find."

The methods by which we try to find a religion to support and guide us must be the same as those that we employ in other fields of life and which are comprehended under the name of science. In this sense we say, the religion we seek is the religion of science.

PRINCIPLES, FAITH, AND DOCTRINES

PRINCIPLES, FAITH, AND DOCTRINES.

What is religion?

Every religion is, or should be, a conviction that regulates man's conduct, affords comfort in affliction, and consecrates all the purposes of life.

What is science?

Science is the methodical search for truth; and truth is a correct, exhaustive, and concise statement of facts.

What is the religion of science?

The religion of science is that religion wherein man aspires to find the truth by the most reliable and truly scientific methods.

The religion of science recognises the authority of truth, scientifically proved, as ultimate. It does not rely on human authority, even though that authority pretends to have special revelations from some supernatural source.

The religion of science accepts no special revelations, yet it recognises certain principles. It has no creed or dogma, yet it has a clearly defined faith. It does not prescribe peculiar ceremonies or rituals, yet it propounds definite doctrines and insists on a rigorous ethical code.

What are the principles of the religion of science?

First, to inquire after truth.
Second, to accept the truth.
Third, to reject what is untrue.
Fourth, to trust in truth.
And fifth, to live the truth.

Is there a difference in principle between religious and scientific truth?

No, there is none.

There is a holiness about science which is rarely appreciated either by priests or by scientists.   Scientific truth is not profane, it is sacred.

There are not two antagonistic truths, one religious, the other scientific.   There is but one truth, which is to be discovered by scientific methods and applied in our religious life.

Truth is one, and the recognition of truth is the basis of all genuine religion.

What are creeds and dogmas?

Creeds and dogmas are such religious doctrines as are propounded without proof, and the acceptance of which is demanded even though they may appear absurd before the tribunal of science.

The principles of the religion of science admit of no creeds, yet the religion of science has a faith.

What is the faith of the religion of science?

The faith of the religion of science is its trust in truth.

The difference between faith and creed is this : creed is a mere belief, faith is a moral attitude. Faith in creeds is the determination to be satisfied with unwarranted or unproved statements. The faith of the religion of science is the conviction that truth can be found, and that truth is the sole redeemer.

There are religious teachers who expressly forbid any investigation of their religious dogmas, and insist that rational inquiry shall not be tolerated in matters of faith. Their faith is called blind faith.

The religion of science rejects blind faith as irreligious and immoral, and preaches that it is our duty to inquire into all the questions that arise in life.

The religion of science is not a religion of indifference ; it does not proclaim that kind of toleration which allows every man to believe and act as he pleases. On the contrary, it proclaims most positive and stern doctrines.

Religious indifference, as fashionable now as it has ever been in certain circles, is detestable to any one who is serious about truth.

Let us have honest belief or honest unbelief, and

abandon that unconcerned apathy of a half-hearted religion.

He that is the first and is the last has said:

"I know thy works, that thou art neither cold nor hot. I would that thou wert cold or hot. So then, because thou art lukewarm, and neither cold nor hot, I will spue thee out of my mouth."

What the Roman church claims to be, the religion of science is. The religion of science is the catholic and orthodox religion.

We do not say that the truth as we know it now is perfect and complete. Not at all. We know comparatively little, and the world is inexhaustible in problems. But we do know that truth can be attained step by step. Inquiry into truth is not only a scientific necessity, it is also a religious duty, and no pious devotion is of the right kind, unless it be accompanied by the spirit of research.

While the religion of science rejects dogmas, it is not without doctrines; its faith is not without substance.

What is the source of the doctrines of its faith?

The doctrines of the religion of science are the result of experience, not of one man only, but of the whole race.

They have to be proved and are always liable to critical revision.

What does the religion of science teach regarding rituals and ceremonies?

The religious life of the established religions consists to a great extent in the use of sacraments, ceremonies, and rituals, symbols instituted to convey in allegorical form religious doctrines, and to express by visible signs and outward forms the invisible spiritual relations between men and God. Baptism, confession, the holy communion, matrimony, are such rituals. The religion of science does not deny that appropriate forms are needed to express in a worthy and adequate way those transactions which are of a religious nature. Ceremonies are one way of consecrating life and the most important events of life. Yet the symbols must adequately express the ideas, and the ideas must be true.

The religion of science attaches no intrinsic value to symbols themselves, but only to their meanings. The symbols must not be conceived as the Indian conceives the spell of the medicine-man. They are meaningless and inefficient aside from the meaning that men put into them. There is no magic power in them. The religion of science has no objection to ceremonies, but it does not prescribe special and peculiar forms as essential to religion, or as indispensable conditions of salvation.

What are the doctrines of the religion of science?

(1) The religion of science propounds as one of its main doctrines that every act has its unavoidable con-

sequences, good or evil, according to the nature of the act. (2) The religion of science teaches that the moral commandments in which almost all the established religions agree are sound. (3) That which is good and that which is evil must be found out by scientific investigation. (4) The religion of science accepts the verdicts of science.

This does not mean that the opinion of every scientist is to be accepted as science, but only those statements which are proved by rational arguments and can be verified by experience, or, if possible, also by experiments.

What is the place of scientists in the religion of science?

Scientists, as seekers of truth, are prophets of the religion of science.

Prophets and priests have authority in the measure in which they represent the authority of moral conduct. They have no authority of themselves. Thus, to the faithful believer no amount of error or fraud in prophets and priests will overthrow their trust in religion.

The same is true of science.

Scientists have authority in such measure as they have investigated, found, and proved the truth. They have no authority of themselves.

Scientists are subject to error, yet no amount of error can overthrow science and the authority of science.

The religion of science is based upon the authority of science, not of scientists, and science is not only physics or the so-called natural sciences, but it includes also sociology and ethics. Scientists as prophets of truth are indispensable helpmates of the preachers of morality. Yet scientists and preachers are mortal, like other human beings, and both of them are liable to error.

As priests are frequently found wanting in religious virtues, so scientific professors are often lacking in the ethics of science.

Scientists object to popes; but how many of them revere their own persons as infallible vicars of truth! And how arrogant, as a rule, how obstinate and per-vicacious is the tenor of their disputes! What stub-born sticklers are they for trifles! How great is their vanity! Happily, there are exceptions. Yet even if there were no exceptions, the authority of science would stand in spite of all the shortcomings of scien-tists.

It is to be conceded that scientific men are always at variance among themselves concerning truths to be discovered. This, however, does not contradict the fact that the truth can be found and clearly stated. Some questions have been settled for good, others are still open. The former are to be regarded as scientific truths. They are such as will be agreed upon by all those who take the trouble to study the subject care-fully. The open questions only are the objects of contention among the searchers for truth, and their very disagreement is a most important means for the discovery of truth.

What is our relation to truth?

Truth is a correct statement of facts and the laws of its being; it describes a power independent of us.

Whether or not truth will be such as we desire it to be, is not the question. We cannot fashion or alter it. Being unalterable, we can only accept it and regulate our life accordingly. There is no choice left for us.

There is no reason, however, to be timid when finding ourselves at the mercy of a power beyond our control. We have developed into thinking, feeling, and aspiring beings, and our rational nature, which appears in its fullest efflorescence in science, enables us to make firm and certain steps. We can combat the evils of life, and better conquer them, the deeper and greater our insight is into truth. The very fact of our existence, such as it is, and the practical importance of truth, inspires us with confidence in that Allbeing, in which and through which we have originated, and the laws of whose nature are beyond our control. We have no choice left but to trust in truth, and we have also good reasons to do so.

*   *   *

It is true that we are surrounded by mysteries, temptations, and afflictions. Yet these conditions of our life urge us the more seriously to search for the truth, lest we go astray and become the victims of our errors. There is certainly no other choice left for us than to take reality as it is, to understand it, and to act in concord with its laws. We cannot make the truth; we cannot fashion it at our pleasure; we can only accept it. But blessed is he who trusts in the truth, who harkens to its behests, and leads a life in which obedience to truth is exemplified.

THE AUTHORITY FOR CONDUCT

THE AUTHORITY FOR CONDUCT.

Is there any authority for conduct? How do we know of it, and what is its nature?

Truth is a correct statement of facts; not of single facts, but of facts in their connection with the totality of other facts, and, finally, with all facts, so that we can see the regularities that obtain as well in one as in other cases; or, popularly speaking, that we can understand their why and wherefore.

Truth, accordingly, is a description of existence under the aspect of eternity (*sub specie æternitatis*). We have to view facts so as to discover in them that which is permanent. We must dig down to that which is immutable and everlasting, to that which will be the same in the present instance as in any other instance, so as to behold in facts the law of their being. We can make or mar almost all objects with which in our experience we come in contact; but that peculiar feature of facts which we describe in laws, the everlasting, the immutable and eternal, that which will be the same in the same conditions, is beyond our control. We cannot alter or fashion it. It is as it is, and we have to mind it in all things which we do or aspire for.

These wonderful features of facts, which we call laws, have shaped the world and man, and the moral ideals of man. They are shaping the fate of the universe still, and will continue to shape it for all time to come. They are the everlasting in nature, and if, in a figurative sense, we personify nature, we can speak of nature's laws as that which constitutes her character.

When reflecting on this peculiar character of reality, we are overawed by its grandeur, but the most wonderful thing about it is that the laws of nature are ultimately not mystical, but easily intelligible.

Science teaches us, step by step, that all laws form a harmonious system of laws. They are all corollaries of an all-pervading regularity. We have to regard all special laws as applications of general laws and learn thus why they must be such as they are and cannot be otherwise.

If science were, or could be perfected to omniscience, the laws of being, we have no reason to doubt, would be pellucid as glass, and even in their most complicated instances as obviously self-evident as $2 \times 2 = 4$, and the all-pervading plan would appear strikingly simple.

Yet how prodigious and portentous are the results of this intrinsic harmony! What strict uniformity and what astonishing variety! What rigidity of law, and yet what a free play for all possible variations! A stringent and irrefragable order in constantly changing conditions!

The everlasting in existence is the ultimate authority for our conduct, and, as such, it has, in the language of religion, been called by the name of God.

The evolution of social beings takes place as all other events of nature according to law, and this law is briefly called the moral law of nature. The moral law is as stern, implacable, and irrefragable as any other law. Wherever it is heeded it will bring blessings ; wherever it is disobeyed it will be followed by curses.

All religious commands are human formulas designed to inform people how to live in accord with the moral law. Not the authority of religious commands, but that of the moral law, is ultimate. Religious commands derive their justification from the moral law of nature. They are right if they are in agreement with it, otherwise they are wrong.

The authority for conduct is a reality, the existence of which can be established by scientific investigation. The moral law of nature is as undeniable as the existence of gravitation and as the reliability of mathematics.

*   *   *

What has science to say of God ?

Science does not speak of God, and need not speak of God, because it employs another terminology than religion. Moreover, it does not search for the eternal of nature in its totality, but in its various and particular manifestations only, and expresses abstractly the results of its investigations in formulas called natural laws.

While science does not speak of God, it teaches God ; for every law of nature is a part of God's being. Every law of nature is in its sphere an authority for conduct ; it is a power which can be adapted to our wants only when we adapt ourselves to it. It is independent of our wishes and cannot be infringed upon with impunity.

All the great religions of the world which (with the sole exception of Buddhism) have called the ultimate authority for conduct " God," have represented him in the image of man. Religious Theism is almost without exception anthropomorphic.

*   *   *

The various views of God are briefly denoted by the following terms :

Theism, or the belief, without any qualification, that God, whatever be his nature, exists.

Atheism, or the view that rejects any conception of God.

Polytheism, or the belief in many gods.

Monotheism, or the belief that there is but one God.

Anthropotheism, or the belief that God is a personal being like man.

Pantheism, or the belief that identifies the All with God.

Deism, or the view adopted by the Freethinkers of the eighteenth century, who rejected miracles, but held that God is a personal being, the Creator and Legislator of the universe.

Entheism, or the view that regards God as insepar- able from the world. He is the eternal in nature.

Which conception of God is adopted by the religion of science?

The religion of science is not Atheistic, but The- istic.

Monotheism, as it is commonly held, is the belief in a single God. In this sense monotheism is actually a polytheism that has reduced its gods to one in num- ber. Yet God is neither one single individual God nor many Gods. Number does not apply to him. God is one not in the sense that there is one kind of Godhood. There is not one God-being; but there is divinity. God is one in the same sense that there is but one reason and but one truth.

The religion of science rejects Anthropotheism and also Deism, which is only a peculiar kind of Anthropo- theism.

The God of the religion of science is not a person. However, he is not less than a person, but infinitely more than a person. The authority for conduct which the religion of science teaches is divine and holy. We should neither call God personal nor impersonal, but superpersonal.

The religion of science does not accept Pantheism. It does not regard nature and all parts of nature or all aspects of nature as identical with God. The eternal of nature only is God. Those features alone are divine which serve us as authority for conduct. We do not look up with reverence to the forces of nature which we utilise, but only to that power which moulds worlds, which fashions our being, and which moves onward in the progress of evolution.

This view we call Entheism.

ETHICS OF THE RELIGION OF SCIENCE

ETHICS OF THE RELIGION OF SCIENCE.

What is the essential difference between religious and irreligious ethics ?

The ethics of the old religions can briefly be characterised as obedience to God, while the ethics of the atheist consists in the attempt to bring about as much happiness as possible.   The former establishes an objective authority of conduct which imposes duties upon us ; while the latter makes the criterion of morality subjective.   The former is briefly called the ethics of duty ; the latter the ethics of pleasure or hedonism.

The religion of science rejects the ethics of pleasure and accepts the ethics of duty.   The authority of conduct is an objective power in the world, a true reality which cares little about our sentiments.   We cannot rely upon our sentiments, our desire for pleasure, our pursuit of happiness, for a correct determination of our duty.

What is the part of happiness in ethics ?

The ethical problem has nothing to do with happiness ; the ethical problem proposes the question, What is our duty ? And our duty remains our duty whether it pleases us or not.

The problem concerning happiness is not, How can we satisfy as much as possible the desires which, we hope, will make us happy, but how shall we learn to be happy while attending to our duty ?

The fact is, that the neglect of our duties causes great misery ; but the attendance to our duties does not by any means always imply an increase of happiness.

What is the purport of happiness ?

Happiness of which men speak so much and which is often so eagerly sought in a wild pursuit, does not at all play an important part in the real world of facts. Nor does it lie in the direction toward which our desires impel us.   Happiness is a mere subjective accompaniment in life which is of a relative nature.

Happiness may be compared to a fraction, the denominator of which consists in our wants and desires ; the numerator, of their satisfactions ; and man's nature is such that their relation remains always a proper fraction.   The denominator is always greater than the numerator ; for as soon as the satisfactions habitually increase, they are accepted as a matter of course ; we become accustomed to them, so that we no longer feel them as pleasures, which means, in the terms of our simile, we at once increase the denominator in equal proportions.

Is there an increase of happiness through evolution?

Duty requires us to aspire forward on the road of progress. But while our pains are constantly lessened and our various wants are more and more gratified, the average happiness does not increase. It rather decreases. The child is, as a rule, happier than the man; and a man of little culture is jollier than a sage. The fool is happy in his foolishness.

Shall we abandon progress, culture, and wisdom, when we learn that our happiness will thereby be diminished?

If hedonism were the right ethical principle, we ought to sacrifice anything for an increase of happiness; but it is not.

Nature does not mind our theories. Our theories must mind nature. We have to grow and to advance, and our happiness is only an incidental feature in the fate of our lives. In considering the duties of life, we should not and we cannot inquire whether our obedience to duty will increase or decrease happiness.

Shall we regard the pursuit of happiness as immoral?

Buddhistic and Christian ethics recognise the futility of the pursuit of happiness. But in misunderstanding the spirit of the will of God, of the authority of conduct, of the moral order of the Universe, some disciples of Buddha and of Christ teach the ethics of asceticism. They regard the pursuit of happiness as immoral.

It is remarkable that neither Buddha nor Christ taught the ethics of asceticism. Buddha expressly declared that self-tormenting was injurious and unnecessary for salvation, and Christ did not request his disciples to fast. He himself ate and drank so that his enemies reproached him with being "a man gluttonous and a wine bibber" (Matth. xi, 19).

What does the religion of science teach of asceticism ?

The ethics of asceticism is the morality of the monk. It is negativism. It aims at the destruction of life.

The religion of science does not accept hedonism, but neither does it accept asceticism. The one is as erroneous as the other.

The religion of science bids us inquire into the duties of life and to attend to them.

Man must study his own self ; he must understand which of his desires are good and which are bad. He must inquire into the nature of the authority of conduct which prescribes duties to him. He must strengthen that part of his soul which aspires to perform duties and even identify his very being with the behests of the authority of conduct : He must become an incarnation of God.

This will teach self-control as the main duty toward one's self and justice as the main duty toward others.

Asceticism may be regarded as an attempt at doing more than duty requires. The ascetic tries to become divine by suppressing or destroying the human.

As soon as we understand that the truly human is a revelation of the divine in nature, we shall see the error of regarding them as antagonistic. By suppressing the human, we suppress the divine.*

Let us not regard that which is truly human as being beneath the dignity of moral aspirations.

The pursuit of happiness is not wrong, and to enjoy the pleasures of life is no sin. It is only wrong to regard happiness as the criterion of ethics and to believe that pleasures are the ultimate aim of life.

* * *

Recreations, pleasures, and aspiring to happiness are not the purposes of life, yet they are in their season not only allowable, but even moral duties. Relaxation is necessary, and happiness imparts a buoyancy which helps man to accomplish his work. A rigorous suppression of our natural inclinations renders us unfit to attend to our duties. There is no virtue in morosity, and the happiness of living creatures, is, as it were, the divine breath which animates them.

Every fact is suggestive, and every truth implies a

---

* In this sense the sentence of Terence is often quoted: " *Nihil humani a me alienum puto.*"

duty.   Our own existence, the relations to our fellow beings, the nature of reality and the constitution of the Universe—in a word, everything teaches us lessons which we have to mind. There are duties toward ourselves, toward our fellow creatures, and toward the future of mankind.

*   *   *

The prescripts of the religion of science keeping aloof from hedonism and from asceticism, may be briefly formulated as follows :

Know thyself and the laws of thy being.

Learn the duties which the laws of thy being imply.

Attend unfalteringly to thy duties.

THE SOUL

THE SOUL.

What am I? Whence dc I come, whither do I go, and what is the substance that constitutes my being?

My fellow-beings appear to me, like all other objects of my surroundings, as material bodies, which are in motion; and so I appear to them and to myself. But the nature of my own self is different. I am a living and feeling being. My own self manifests itself in consciousness. I am aware of my own existence; and the whole range of my existence in so far as I am directly aware of it, is called the soul.

What is the nature of our soul?

Our soul consists of impulses, dispositions, and ideas. I am a living, willing, and thinking being.

Impulses are tendencies to act, naturally called forth in irritable substance by all kinds of stimuli. Habits are acquired by the frequent repetition of impulses. Impulses grown strong by inveterate habits are called passions.

Inherited habits constitute dispositions or propensities which awake to activity on the slightest provocation. They form the foundation of the various functions of the organs of the organism, and also of the tenor of conscious soul-life. The latter is generally called temperament.

Ideas are representations of things, or of qualities of things, or of relations among things. When ideas enter into the causation of action as the determinant element, they are called motor-ideas or motives.

The elementary impulses of our soul are not clearly and distinctly perceived. They mingle into one common sensation, which is quite general and vague. Sometimes only by special disturbances do some of the elementary impulses rise into prominence, appearing as hunger or thirst or pain of some kind.

The realm of the activity of our elementary impulses constitutes what we feel as our life.

Every impulse is a tendency to move; and in so far as impulses are called forth by stimuli which act upon the living substance, they are called "reactions."

As soon as impulses become clearly conscious they are called will. Will, accordingly, is a very complex kind of impulse. Will is an impulse in which a clear conception of the result of the motion constitutes the main factor of the tendency to move. In other words, will is an impulse which has developed into a motor-idea.

How do ideas originate?

Ideas develop out of feelings.

That which characterises the soul of thinking beings,

is the significance which its feelings possess. Certain sensations are produced by certain stimuli, the same sensations always by the same stimuli; and these peculiar forms of various feelings become indicators of the presence of the various conditions that cause them. Thus they acquire meaning, and meaning produces clearness. Meaning changes dim feelings into consciousness.

The origin of meaning in feelings is the birth of mind.

Sensations which take place inside the organism are, through habits and inherited dispositions, projected to the outside, where experience has taught us to expect them. Sensations are signs, indicating objective realities, and when through the mechanism of language sentient beings develop word-symbols, which are signs of signs, representing whole classes of realities, they rise into the sphere of human existence.

What is thought? What is rational thought? What is reason?

The interaction which takes place between ideas is called thought.

All sensations enter into relations with the memories of former sensations; and thus sentient beings naturally develop into thinking beings. Human thought which discovers and utilises the presence of universal features in reality is called rational thought; reason being the norm of correct thinking.

The soul consists of many various impulses, but it possesses at the same time a peculiar unity. How are we to account for the unity of the soul?

A man can think incompatible ideas, but he cannot act according to them, at least not at the same time. He can, to be sure, successively obey motives that are self-contradictory, but he will have to stand the consequences; so that a man will have to regret his actions as soon as wiser and better ideas become dominant in his soul.

The necessity of action imperatively imposes upon the soul a unity which would otherwise scarcely originate. The whole organism has to act as a unity; conflicting impulses and contradictory ideas must come to an agreement. And thus the necessity of harmonious action exercises a wholesome and educating influence. It tests ideas in practical issues; it matures them by bringing incompatible motor-ideas into conflict, thus establishing consistency in the soul.

If situations arise in which several various impulses and conflicting motor-ideas tend to be realised in action, a struggle will begin among them and continue until the strongest one gains the upper hand. This strongest motive, then, is executed by the organism.

The power of passions is all but irresistible in the savage, while rational ideas gradually gain in strength with the advance of civilisation. Long experience, inherited habits, and to a great extent, also, repeated regret for rash actions, accustom man to act only after sufficient and careful deliberation.

The habit of suppressing passions until all conflicting motor-ideas have measured their forces against each other becomes easier and easier, and its exercise is called self-control.

The character of a soul depends upon the impulses and motor-ideas that are dominant in it. They are the decisive elements which determine the actions of a man.

The decision which is the final outcome of deliberation is comparable to a motion carried in a legislative body. It is like the majority vote adopting a plan upon the execution of which the whole body of voters is now resolved, and these resolutions of the soul are called the will of man.

What is the name of the unity of man's soul?

The idea which represents the organism as a whole is called the "I" or ego, and it is a matter of course that the I or ego always regards the final outcome of deliberations as its own resolutions.

The ego, by itself, is an empty symbol. Its contents are those which the ego stands for, viz., the qualities of the whole soul; that is, of the impulses and motor-ideas of the personality which the ego represents.

We say, "I have ideas"; but we ought to say, "I consist of ideas." My ideas are real parts of myself.

The phrase, "I have an idea," can only mean that this idea stands in connection with the ego-idea, representing the whole personality of myself. It is at the moment present in the focus of consciousness.

The contents of the ego of a man, viz., the constituents of his personality, are changeable. He wills now this, now that, and his actions at different times are often very incompatible with each other. But there is a continuity in his acts which is recorded in a chain of memories called recollections, in all of which the acting person regards himself as a constant factor and is called by the same pronoun "I." The expression "I" being for a continuous series of acts the same in spite of many changes, produces the illusion that the acting person himself remains the same throughout.

However, we know for certain that the acting person, our organism, and the ideas of which we consist, do by no means remain unchanged. In the same way that our surroundings change, so we ourselves, our thoughts and desires, our organism, and our very souls change. We call the rose-bush which blooms in June, and is a dry, thorny stick in December, the same rose-bush. We call our body the same body, although the materials of which it consists are comparable to a complex whirl of atoms, the unity of which consists in the preservation of its form, for new materials are constantly pouring in, while part of the old ones pass out. And finally, we call our spiritual self by the same name "I," viewing it as a unity so long as the continuity of its existence is preserved, although our ideas do not remain the same, either in strength or in their contents. The changes in our character at an advanced age may be comparatively slight, but there are, nevertheless, changes, which are not less real because they remain unheeded. Our self being the measure of things, they appear to change when we change, and we seem to remain the same; yet this unalterable sameness of our self is a fiction.

There is an error very prevalent that the ego-idea is the real soul. The existence of an ego-soul, however, has been abandoned by science. Need we add that all those whose views and sentiments are closely intertwined with the conception of an ego-soul, look upon its surrender as a destruction of the very root of religion and of all religious hopes?

What is the effect upon religion of surrounding the conception of an ego-soul?

Our conception of the nature of the human soul has been as thoroughly altered through the results of modern scientific research as our view of the universe since the times of Copernicus. Copernicus abandoned the geocentric, and psychology the egocentric standpoint; and future religious development will be influenced in no less a degree by the latter than it has been by the former.

New truths appear at first sight always appalling. They come to destroy the errors which we have ac-

customed ourselves to cherish as truths. Thus the
truth naturally appears to be destructive. But look at
the truth closer, and you will find that it is after all
better and greater and nobler than the most beautiful
fiction woven of errors.

Appalling, and destructive of the very foundations
of our religious conceptions, as the surrender of the
ego may seem at first sight, a closer acquaintance with
the subject will show that the scientific solution of the
problem of soul-life does not annihilate but elevates
and purifies religion. It dispels the mystery of religious
doctrines and preserves their ethical kernel.

There is no metaphysical ego-soul, yet there is the
real soul of our ideas and ideal aspirations, and the
value of the latter is not less because the former has
proved to be an error.

All the religious enthusiasm which men have pro-
fessed to have for their ego-souls, and of which they
have proved the earnestness in deeds, expresses the
natural sentiments for their real souls.

Facts are often misinterpreted, and misinterpreted
facts are rejected by many. We must reject the mis-
interpretation and accept the facts.

The welfare of our souls is the mission, or rather
the ultimate object of life ; for what shall it profit a
man if he gain the whole world and lose his own soul ?

How shall we value souls ?

The worth of a man does not consist in his titles,

not in the honors he receives from his fellow-men, not in his possessions, not in his knowledge nor in his talent, not in any of the externalities of his life, but in his soul; and the soul of the poorest servant is not less than the soul of the wealthiest man, the most learned savant, or the most powerful monarch. Indeed, the soul in the bosom of the serf that is of the sterling quality of an Epictetus is, without qualification, superior to the soul of a Nero, in spite of the dazzling talents, which made this imperial monster, in the beginning of his reign, appear as a genius on the throne.

We do not say that worldly possessions are worthless, nor do we consider knowledge and talents as an indifferent adjunct; on the contrary, all the gifts and blessings of life possess their values, for they are instrumental, and almost all of them are, in a greater or less degree, indispensable for the furthering and quickening of the life of the soul.

Yet the worth of a soul depends first of all upon the moral stamina of a man's character, and the nobility of the sentiments that dominate his being.

IMMORTALITY

IMMORTALITY.

Is the life of our soul limited?

Every personality consists of a definite idiosyncracy, of impulses, dispositions and motor-ideas, the peculiarity and relative strength of which admit of innumerable variations. Now the question arises, Whence do the constituent elements of a man's soul come, what is the part they play, and whither do they go?

Our soul is partly inherited from our ancestors, (our dispositions,) partly planted in us by education, (in the main our ideas,) partly acquired by imitation, (our habits,) partly formed under the impression of our own individual experience, (in the main our convictions,) and partly worked out through reflection, (in the main our theories). Thought, i. e., the interaction that takes place among the elements of the soul, enables us to make new thought-combinations out of the stock of ideas that live in our mind. Thought renders the anticipation of future facts possible.

Our soul, accordingly, has a long history, which neither begins with our birth, nor ends with our death. We existed wherever the ideas of which we consist were thought, and shall exist wherever they are thought

again ; for not only our body is our self, but mainly our
ideas.   Our true self is of a spiritual nature.

Our life is only a phase in the evolution of a greater
whole, and the spiritual existence of ourselves, our
soul, is a precious inheritance of the past, which will
evolve in future generations to higher and ever higher
planes of being and to nobler and ever nobler desti-
nies.

I.
*   *

The preservation of soul-life after the death of the
individual is not an assumption, nor a probability,
nor a mere hypothesis, but a scientific truth which
can be proved by the surest facts of experience.   If
soul-life were not preserved, evolution would be impossible. Evolution is possible only because the souls
of our ancestors continue to live in us.   The soul of
every individual is a peculiar idiosyncrasy of his ancestors, and of the education received from parents
and teachers.   During his life he adds his own ex-
periences, good or bad, and when he dies his soul is
gathered to his fathers, and together with their souls
it floats on in the great stream of immortality

The continuance of our soul-life beyond death has
been expressed in many different ways. In the mysteries of Eleusis it was allegorically represented by a
torch which went from hand to hand and by ears of
wheat that symbolised the reappearance of vegetation
after its wintery sleep ; while Christianity expresses it
in the dogma of the resurrection of the body.

Among Benjamin Franklin's manuscripts was found an epitaph which he had written in 1728, when he was twenty-three years of age. The many corrections found on the page were added, as we may fairly suppose, in later years, and show that Franklin had pondered on the subject, and that he had given much thought to it. The epitaph* runs as follows :

" The Body

of

BENJAMIN FRANKLIN

Printer

(Like the cover of an old book

Its contents torn out

And stript of its lettering and gilding)

Lies here food for worms.

But the work shall not be lost

For it will [as he believed] appear once more

In a new and more elegant edition

Revised and corrected

by

The Author."

The simile that compares man to a book is very expressive, as it sets the nature of the soul in a true light. We are inclined to regard the binding, the pa-

---

* We may add that Franklin did not make use of this proposed epitaph. He directed in his last will to have a simple stone with nothing on it but the names of himself and his wife. The passage in the testament reads thus :

" I wish to be buried by the side of my wife, if it may be, and that a marble stone, to be made by Chambers, six feet long, four feet wide, plain, with only a small moulding round the upper edge, and this inscription :

BENJAMIN ⎫
AND   ⎬ FRANKLIN.
DEBORAH ⎭   178–

be placed over us both."

per, the presswork as the essential elements of the book; yet we must be aware that they are not its soul.

The soul of the book is its contents. That All-being, in whom we live and move and have our being, publishes one edition after the other, and when one copy is destroyed, the book itself, i. e., the soul of the book, is not lost. If but the contents of the book are valuable, if they contain truth, it will reappear in a new edition, perhaps in a more elegant binding, but certainly revised and corrected and enlarged.

What are the contents of the soul?

The contents of the soul form, in a word, a world-picture, the most important part of which, for human beings, is the relations that obtain and that ought to obtain in human society.

The world-picture of the soul, however, is not a mere image of our surroundings painted in glowing sensations. Man forms a systematic conception of the facts of nature so as to behold the laws of their being.

The world of which we are parts is permeated by law. All events are concatenated and interrelated by causation, and every act of ours has its definite consequences. Through a long process of evolution we have come to be what we are. Our surroundings have impressed themselves upon our sentiency and have moulded all our ideas and the motives that prompt us to act. Our ideas and motives are the quintessence of our being; they are our veriest self, our soul. If and in so far as our ideas are true and our motives right, they are the highest and best and most precious part of our existence, they are the divinity of our being, they are the incarnation of God in us, they are the soul of our soul.

Is there a prototype of the soul?

Rational beings here upon earth might, in many respects, have developed otherwise than they did. It is not impossible that rational creatures on various other planets are in possession of different physical constitutions than we. They may have developed wings; they may have tongs-like organs unlike our hands for taking hold of things, etc., etc. Yet it is certain that they cannot develop another kind of reason. Their arithmetic, their mathematics, their logic must be the same as ours. Nay, more than this, the basic maxims of their ethics cannot be essentially different from those which are the factors underlying the growth and evolution of human society upon earth. In other words : The constitution of the universe is such that certain features of man's soul are necessarily such as they are and cannot be different in any other kind of rational beings. There are not prototypes of beings, as Plato maintained, but there is, nevertheless, something analogous to prototypes. The nature of rational beings is foreordained and conditioned by the very nature of things, and thus the biblical saying appears in a new light, that man has been created in the image of God.

The eternal in nature, the universal in the changes of the world, the law that pervades facts, has taken its abode in man; briefly, it is the truth which appears in his soul, and the truth is a correct representation of reality, it is a picture of God.

Religious truth is not merely a scientific cognition of the parts of the world and a comprehension of all the details of natural laws; it is a comprehension of our being in its relation to the whole, to God. And this comprehension must not be theoretical, it must permeate all our sentiments, it must dominate our entire being and find expression in all the acts of our life.

Why is the scientific view of the soul not readily accepted?

There is one great difficulty in this theory of the soul, of its divinity and of its immortality, as the religion of science propounds it. There is no difficulty about its truth. We can readily see that it is undeniable; it can be positively proved. The facts upon which it rests are beyond dispute. But the difficulty is of another nature. We have great trouble, not so much in understanding, but in feeling that our soul is not our individual self, but God in us.

We are so engrossed with materialism that we look upon the externalities of life as our real self, and this materialism finds expression in the forms of traditional religions now. The binding, paper, and general appearance of a book is in the sight of most people that which constitutes its essential and entire being. Man finds it very hard to rise in his emotional life to that purity of abstraction which distinguishes between the contents or soul, and the present make-up or body, of a book, of a man, of ourselves.

The question of immortality is a moral question. It requires a man of moral fibre to see the solution in its right light. It is not enough to understand the problem ; we must live it. Our natural habits still tend to regard the unessential of our bodily existence as our real self, and all our emotions, our hopes and fears are exclusively attached to this present copy of our soul.

We have not only to change the mode of our thinking, but also the mode of our feeling. We must develop the higher emotions, which are in sympathy with the true essence of our being. We must unlearn the errors that make us lay too much stress upon incidents that have only a passing value, and we must regulate our actions from the standpoint of our spiritual nature. We must feel ourselves to be not the make-up of the present edition of our soul, but the soul itself.

What is the natural standpoint of the unreflecting man ?

That attitude of a man in which, heedless of his soul, he takes his present make-up as his true self is called egotism ; and the man with egotistic tendencies views the world from a standpoint which does not show matters in a correct perspective.

The whole world and his own self are pictured to the egotist in distorted proportions. All his feelings, his sympathies, and antipathies, too, become perverted.

Why must we abandon the standpoint of egotism?

It is apparent that all the purposes of a man which are designed to serve his egotistic desires only, will be vain, and if he were ever so successful in his efforts, death will step in at last and annihilate the very purpose for which he lived.

Nature does not want egotism. She suffers it with forbearance, leaving a man time to find the narrow road to life, but then she cuts him down and selects from the harvest which he had gathered in for himself that which she can use for the progress of mankind, leaving him only the bitter knowledge that the fruits of his work are taken from him and that he has sowed what another shall reap.

Unless a man's entire emotional life be centred in his soul, his life will be a failure.

Is the abandonment of the egoistic standpoint a resignation?

This view of the soul appears to those who still cling to the conception of an ego-soul as a resignation ; and in a certain sense it is a resignation. We have to give up the idea that our real self belongs to ourselves. Our soul is not our own, but mankind's ; and mankind in its turn is not its own ; the soul of mankind is from God, it develops in God, and all its aspirations and yearnings are to God.

Yet the characterisation of this view of the soul as a resignation will produce an erroneous impression. There is as little resignation about it as when in a fairy-tale a shepherd-lad finds out that he is a prince. The resignation consists in resigning an error for truth. What we regarded as our self is not our self, but only a fleeting shadow, and our true self is much greater than we thought it was. The shepherd-boy in the fairy-tale might with the same reason say that his very existence had been wiped out, as some psychologists speak of the annihilation of the soul, when only the ego-conception of the soul is surrendered.

When our sphere of being becomes widened we should not speak of annihilation, and when we grow beyond that which at first blush we seem to be, we should not represent it as a resignation.

He who regards this view of the soul as a resignation only indicates that his sympathies, his hopes and fears are still with the externalities of our existence. The moment the very consciousness of our selfhood is transferred into our soul-existence, we shall cease to feel any resignation in this change of view.

What objection is made to the abandonment of the ego-soul ?

The objection has been raised that there is neither satisfaction nor justice in the idea that others shall reap the fruits of our labors. But this objection has sense only from the standpoint of an ego-conception of the soul. The truth is that the future generations of mankind are not "others"; they are we ourselves. We have inherited in the same way not only the blessings of former generations, but their very being, their souls: we are their continuance.

It is not an empty phrase to say that the former generations of mankind are still alive as a part of ourselves. For suppose that the soul-life of the past were entirely annihilated and no vestige of it left, would not our own existence at once sink to the level of mere amœboid existence? The thought of this will convince us how truly real is the continuance of soul-life after death! The souls of our beloved are always with us and will remain among us until the end of the world.

What does the new conception of the soul imply?

Our spiritual nature imposes duties upon us; it teaches us to regard our life as a phase only of a greater and a more complete evolution, and commands us to rise above the narrowness of our transient and limited existence.

As soon as we rise above the pettiness of our individual being, the boundaries of birth and death vanish, and we breathe the air of immortality. But this change of standpoint is of great consequence. It affects our entire existence and brings about a radical change of our world-conception. It is like a new birth which will above all be felt in our conduct. The higher standpoint of immortality introduces a new principle which will almost reverse our former habits and introduce a new criterion of what is to be regarded as right or wrong.

The moral commandments are rules of action which appear as a matter of course to him who has been born again, who has raised himself to the higher plane of soul-life, and whose sentiments and expressions of this attitude are what Christianity calls " love."

The moral commandments are forced upon the egotist, and the egotist naturally regards them as impositions. However, he whose attitude is that of love, does not feel in this way. He fulfils the commandments of his own free will.

Our sympathies must be the sympathies of our better self, and if they are, our course of action will, without any interference of the law, lead us to do anything the law and the rules of equity demand.

There is no resignation in truly moral conduct. Moral conduct should be the expression of our character; it should flow naturally from the nature of our being.

II.

Immortality is the most important of all religious topics, and it appears desirable to consider the most stringent objections that can be made against it.

Dr. Robert Lewins,* a radical freethinker of Eng-

* See *Agnostic Journal*, XXXIV, No. 26, and *The Open Court*, No. 360.

land, arraigns the Religion of Science for its acceptance of a belief in God and in Immortality, saying :

" The assumption is utterly untenable, though held by Kant,
Voltaire, Rousseau, and even, though more obscurely, by Frederick the Great and David Hume, whose influence on the litera-
ture, history, and politics of their age was so conspicuous.   Spite
of his vast culture, and probably as its consequence, a remnant
of chromatic metaphysics still seems to cling to Dr. Carus."

"This chromatic metaphysics is," according to
Dr. Lewins, "a barrier to achromatic reality," and he
demands that "all forms of Spiritualism or Animism,
including Theism, Demonism, and posthumous human
existence, must be relegated to the sphere of our racial
credulity and superstition."

Now we agree with Dr. Lewins in the aspiration of
having reality as achromatic as possible, but declare
at the same time that a flat denial of "posthumous
human existence" is an error.   The continuance of
man's soul as described in the Religion of Science is
not a coloring of facts, it is not chromatic, it is not a
distortion of truth, but it is an exact statement of the
conditions of life as they are in reality.

Some time ago the following two questions concerning immortality were put to me :

" Do you believe in the survival of man as a distinct individuality after bodily dissolution ?

" Do you believe that man after such bodily dissolution, can,
as a distinct, conscious, intelligent being communicate with those
who still live in the flesh ? "

My reply was this :

" In answer to the first question I should say : I understand by individuality not only man's soul, viz., his sensations, thoughts, and ideals, but his entire existence, including his bones, muscles, sinews, and all the material particles of which at a given time his body consists. Accordingly, I believe in the final dissolution of his individuality, and count it no loss ; but I believe at the same time in the survival of the most essential part of man's individuality, I believe in the survival of man's soul.

"To the second question I should answer: Not only do the souls of our dead continue to communicate with those who still live in the flesh, but they are present in their minds, and they will form parts of the souls of the generations to come. The relation between the dead and the living is too intimate to be called a communication. The souls of the dead form an ever-living presence in the souls of the living. Progress and evolution to higher stages is only possible because the souls of former generations continue to live. If the souls of our ancestors were not with us and in us, what a wretched, and, indeed, merely amœboid existence would we lead."

There is not an iota of metaphysicism or animism left in this view of immortality. But perhaps my critic will say that this is no immortality ; that this is a proposition which teaches the final annihilation of man's personality in death. If he does, he is blind to facts and fails to recognise the importance of that which survives of us, which is not a mere trace of us, but the essence of our personality, our very soul, the substance and worth of our being.

In one sense, transiency is the order of the universe, in another sense, permanency. The present

changes into the past, never to be the present again;
it passes away. Every happening in the physical
world takes place never to happen again in exactly
the same way and under the very same circumstances.
But being embodied in the past, it remains an actual
part of the constitution of the world. It has become
a factor for all the future, and will be a determinant
of any possible present to come. In the same way
every act of ours passes away, yet it is immortalised:
it remains an indelible reality of our life, influencing
and shaping our fate. Every thought of ours once
thought and buried in the past of former years is, in a
certain sense, gone forever, but in another sense, it
remains an everpresent reality, and our soul is a grand
structure consisting of the immortalised precipitate of
the sentiments, ideas, and acts done in past years,
dating back to the beginning of soul-life upon earth.

What is true of all events in the physical world
and of the facts of our psychical existence, is true also
of whole human lives. Nothing is lost in this world,
least of all a human soul. To be gathered to our
fathers does not mean to be buried in the ground, but
to be embodied as a living element into the evergrow-
ing organism of mankind. There we are preserved as
a living presence with all our peculiarities and with
the entire personality of our being. Death is a dissolution of our body; it is the end of our career; it is
the discontinuance of our activity in this individuality
of ours. Yet is it no annihilation of our thoughts, of

our soul, of our spiritual existence, of ourselves. Deeds
live on; and what are we but the summation of our
deeds! Our deeds, that is to say, we ourselves, continue
after death as much as the memory of a useful knowledge which we have learned in the days of our youth
remains an essential part of us throughout life.

Thus we may lament the premature cutting off of
a valuable life by death, but we cannot complain about
the annihilation of a man's soul; for it continues, it is
here with us and in us. We might as well complain
of the transiency of our school-years, forgetful of the
fact that both the knowledge we have acquired and
the fond recollections of dear friends are permanent.

The past lives on in the present and the dead continue in the living. Every soul is and remains for ever
a citizen of that invisible empire of spiritual existence
which is always coming, always near at hand, and always developing and growing. This empire of spiritual
life is not a phantom but an actuality. If anything is
real, *it* is real. It is the kingdom of God of which
Jesus said that it is within us.

Now, in the face of facts and in the face of the important part which the continuance of the soul plays
in our life, shall we at the funeral of our dead step
forward and preach the annihilation of their existence?
Shall we say at the open grave of a friend that the belief in immortality is a remnant of metaphysics and
animism to be relegated to the sphere of superstition?
No! Spiritual facts are not less real than rocks and

trees. Immortality is a truth as much as the existence
of man's soul; and a denial of it will warp our entire
world-conception.

As it is difficult for the uneducated mass of mankind to recognise the reality of the truth of immortality
and to appreciate its paramount importance, the various
religions have taught it in allegories which in Christianity have been crystallised into the dogma of resurrection. The doctrine of resurrection is a parable, and
the parable contains allegorical expressions which are
crude and inappropriate; but the idea contained in it
is a truth. Science rejects the assumption of a ghost-
soul and also of a ghost-immortality, but science establishes at the same time the reality of the continuance
of man's soul after death.

The immortality of the soul as taught by the Religion of Science is as complete and full as any faithful
Christian can reasonably expect. It is as real as the
continuance of our self which we daily experience. It
is not of less value, but of more value than the ghost-
immortality of an impossible dualism; it is not ghastly,
not grotesque, not absurd (as Dr. Lewins says), but
noble, elevating, and comforting.

The immortality of the soul, such as the Religion
of Science proposes, is right here in this actual world
of ours, not in a celestial Utopia; it is real and not il-
lusory; it is a fact and not a dream; it is an undeniable truth and not, as Voltaire, Frederick the Great,
and his friends thought, a grand *peut être.*

MYTHOLOGY AND RELIGION

`

MYTHOLOGY AND RELIGION.

What is the attitude of the religion of science towards other religions?

The religion of science is not hostile to the spirit of the traditional religions: on the contrary, being their matured product, it regards them as harbingers that prepare the way.

The dogmatic religions are mythologies which attempt to teach the truth in parable and allegory. They are prophecies of the religion of truth.

Is mythology injurious?

Mythology in itself is not injurious; on the contrary, it is a necessary stage in the evolution not only of religion, but also of science. Man's mode of conveying thought is essentially mythological. All language is based upon similes and we shall perhaps never be able to speak without using figures of speech.

The religion of science does not come to destroy the mythologies of old religion; it does not come to destroy but to fulfil.

What is the nature of the mythology of science?

Science no less than religion had to pass and, in many of its fields, is still passing, through a mythological period; and this mythological period is often marked by fantastic notions and extravagant vagaries. Astrology preceded astronomy, and alchemy preceded chemistry.

It is a great mistake of the chemist to look down upon the alchemist, and of the astronomer to speak with contempt of the astrologer of former ages. It is a sign either of narrowness or of a lack of information to revile our ancestors because they knew less than we. Baron Liebig was the greatest chemist of his times; yet he speaks with profound respect of the aspirations and accomplishments of the alchemists. Those upon whose shoulders we stand deserve our thanks not our contempt. Let us not despise the anthropoid from whose labors man has risen to the height of a human existence !

The mythology of science still clings to us to-day.

When does mythology become injurious ?

Mythology becomes injurious as soon as it is taken as the truth itself.

Mythology thus produces that self-sufficient spirit of dogmatism which prevents further inquiry into truth.

What is the origin of the mythological religions ?

The historical religions were founded at a time when science and its methods of inquiry did not as yet exist. Yet religion was wanted. People cannot live without spiritual support and solace and guidance. And as the old Egyptians instinctively discovered such tools as the lever and other simple instruments helpful to them in their work long before they understood the principles of these contrivances ; as mankind in general instinctively invented language as a means of communication without having any philological knowledge, and even without the least inkling of the laws of grammar and logic: so some prophets rose among our ancestors preaching to them some simple rules of conduct which they had instinctively found when pondering on the miseries caused by criminal and ruthless behavior.

The nobler conduct, preached by prophets and enforced by the evil consequences of sin, raised mankind to a higher ground. Men learned to feel and appreciate the truth of the religious authority which proclaims the moral commands; and the religious convictions thus established proved even in their imperfect form an invaluable source of solace and help in the tribulations of life.

Does the law of evolution apply to religion also ?

Religion develops according to natural laws. Not only the human body and all living creatures, but also such intangible and spiritual entities as science, law, language, and social institutions are products of evolution, and religion forms no exception.

The hypotheses of science are often formulated with the help of analogies, and these analogies contain figurative expressions. We speak for instance of elec-

tric currents, as if electricity were a fluid. This method
of using analogies which is of great service in scientific
investigations must not be taken as real science : it is
the mythology of science.

The mythology of science is no less indispensable
in the realm of investigation than it is in the province
of religion ; but we must not forget that it is a means
only to an end, the ideal of scientific inquiry being and
remaining a simple statement of facts.

While we may be able to free ourselves from the
shackels of mythology in science and philosophy, must
we, perhaps, still retain them in religion ?

The progress of religion in this direction will be the
same as in science and philosophy.

Progress of science means the formation of new
ideas, and the purification of our old ones. The mythological elements must be separated from the pure
statement of facts, the latter being the grain, the former the chaff ; the latter are the truth, the former our
mythologies, being the methods of reaching the truth.

The chaff is the husks, and grain cannot grow without the wholesome protection of the husks. The truth
contained in mythological allegories is their all-im-
portant element, which has to be sifted out and preserved.   The rest is to be discarded ; it has served an
educational purpose and will have to be relegated to
the history of science.

Religious progress, no less than scientific progress,

is a process of growth, it is an increment of truth, and also a cleansing from mythology.

Religion is a world-conception regulating man's conduct. Our world-conception grows with every new information, and all those new ideas from which we derive moral rules of conduct become religious ideas.

As science began with the crude notions of primitive animism, so did religion begin with a mythology full of superstition. And the ideal of religion is the same as that of science, it is an increase of truth as well as a liberation from mythological elements. The more complete our knowledge is, the less is our need of hypotheses, and mythological expressions can be replaced by exact statements of fact. Both science and religion are to be based upon a concise but exhaustive statement of facts, which is to be constantly enlarged by a more complete and more accurate experience.

The ultimate goal of religious development is the recognition of the truth with the aspiration to live in conformity to the truth.

Mythology which is conceived to be the truth itself is called paganism.

Paganism is the notion that the parable is the meaning it involves, that the letter is the spirit, that mythology is the truth.

It is certainly no error to believe that virtue, justice, beauty, love, and other ideas have a real and true existence in reality. They whose spiritual eyes are too dim to see and to understand their being, will be greatly benefited by the representations of the artist and the poet, who present those ideals to us, the latter in our imagination, the former visibly in marble as personal beings, as gods.   There is no wrong in similes, there is no fault to be found with parables.   But he who believes that these gods are personal beings, he who takes the mythology to be the actual truth, is under the spell of a gross misconception, and this misconception is paganism.

Paganism leads to idolatry.   He who worships the symbol is an idolater.

The dogmatic religions of to-day are still under the spell of paganism ; and even Christianity, the highest, the noblest, and most humane of all religions, is not yet free of idolatry,—a fact which appears in many various customs and ceremonies. Sacrifices have been abandoned, but prayer, adoration, and other institutions still indicate the pagan notion that God is like a human being, that he takes delight in receiving honors, and that upon special considerations he will change his decrees and reverse the order of nature for the sake of those whom he loves.

The religion of science does away with paganism and idolatry.

The religion of science rejects the religion of adoration, and prescribes only one kind of worship—the worship in spirit and in truth which consists in obeying the authority of moral conduct.

The religion of science rejects all the vain repetitions of such prayers as attempt to change not our will but the will of God. Those prayers only are admitted by the religion of science which set our souls in harmony with the authority of conduct, which consists in self-discipline and teach us to say with Jesus of Nazareth " Not our, but Thy will be done ! "

What are the sources of religious truth?

The religion of science knows of no special revelations; it recognises only the revelation of truth, open to all of us, as it appears in our experience, viz., in the events of nature surrounding us, and also in the emotions of our own heart.

Religion is not due to a supernatural revelation, but to the same natural revelation to which science owes its existence.

The form of the established religions is mythological, for its founders spoke in parables, and the allegorical form of their teachings was quite adapted to the age in which they lived.

New problems have arisen with the growth of science. The mythology of our religions has become palpably untenable, and we are no longer satisfied with the dogmas extracted from parables.

Is there any conflict between religion and science?

True science and true religion can never come in conflict. If there is any conflict between religion and science, it is a sign that there is something wrong in either our science or our religion, and we shall do well to revise them both.

This is the conflict that at present obtains between science and religion. The infidel laughs at the impostures of religion, while the bigot demands an implicit surrender of reason.

The infidel as well as the bigot are under the erroneous impression that the mythology of religion is religion itself.

What is to be done?

The bigot demands that science be muzzled, and the infidel proposes to eradicate religion.

Shall we follow the bigot who wants the errors of paganism to continue? Or shall we follow the infidel? Shall we root out science, because it is not as yet free from mythology? Shall we eradicate mankind because there are traces of barbarism left in our institutions, even to-day? Shall we abandon religion because it still retains some of the superstitious notions of paganism?

We follow neither the bigot nor the infidel, but propose confidently to advance on the road of progress. It is the course prescribed by nature, which willingly or unwillingly we shall have to pursue.

The ideal towards which every religious evolution tends, is to develop a Religion of Truth. And this ideal can be reached only through an honest search for the truth with the assistance of the scientific methods of inquiry.

Christianity possesses an ideal which is called "the invisible church." Even the most devout Christians are aware of the fact that the present condition of the church is not the realisation of its ideal. The ideal of the invisible church can find its realisation only in the religion of science.

CHRIST AND THE CHRISTIANS;
A CONTRAST

CHRIST AND THE CHRISTIANS; A CONTRAST.

For the sake of convenience, let us distinguish between Christ and Jesus. While the name Jesus denotes an historical man, who, as we have good reason to believe, lived about two thousand years ago, we understand by Christ that ideal figure, which has been the main factor in forming the Christian church and which is represented in the gospels.

Whether Jesus was Christ, in other words, whether the account of the gospels is historical or mythical, is a problem which we do not care to discuss in detail here. The problem is of a purely scientific nature and has nothing to do with practical religion, except as it may open the eyes of those who are as yet under the spell of the paganism which still prevails in our churches.* It is quite immaterial whether or not the accounts of the

---

* The problem of Jesus can now be regarded as solved, and the results of all the laborious researches into the accounts of the gospels have been summed up by H. Holtzmann, Professor of Theology at the University of Strassburg i. E., in his *Hand-Commentar sum neuen Testament.* Professor Holtzmann's works are the more valuable as they are the statement, not of a Freethinker, but of a Christian and a theologian by profession. They are reverent, but scientific and critical.

Holtzmann's results remain positive. Jesus is, in his opinion, an historical person, whose human character and fate can best be traced in Mark, the oldest of the gospels.

gospel are historical ; yet it is not a matter of indifference whether or not the Christ-ideal is true ; and we
say that it is true ; and so far as its truth has been recognised, the spirit of Christ lives and moves and has
its being.

The belief in the miraculous, which existed at the
time of Christ, quite naturally entered into the gospels, and we cannot regard it as an absolutely injurious element, whose presence ought to be deplored.
On the contrary, miracles and the belief in miracles
indicate the power of the Christ-ideal. All great historical movements are soon surrounded by more or
less beautiful legends, and these legends frequently
reflect the meaning of history better than the historical facts themselves, for the legends reveal to us, in a
poetical vision, the thriving power of historical movements. There we peep, as it were, into the minds of
mankind ; we see their yearning, aspiring, wondering,
and we learn their conception of the ideals that move
in their hearts. Christianity would have been insignifi-
cant and insipid, if it had not produced such a mythology as we possess now. There is no fault to be found
with the mythology, but only with those who misun-
derstand the part which mythologies play in the evolution of religious ideas.

We have to accept the results of science in its investigation of the historical pretensions of the gospels, yet at the same time we insist on the fact that
Christ is a living presence even to-day, and our whole

civilisation is pervaded by his spirit. Christ is the key-note of the historical evolution of mankind since the second century of the Christian era, and it seems improbable that the influence of this ideal will ever subside, or that its glory will ever be outshone by a greater star to come ; for the Christ-ideal is a tendency, rather than a type ; it indicates the direction of moral progress, and not a special aim ; it represents an aspiration towards perfection, and not a fixed standard. Thus, with all moral rigidity, nay, sternness, with all definiteness and stability, the Christ-ideal combines an extraordinary plasticity ; it is capable of evolution, of expansion, of growth.

Christ is an invisible and superpersonal influence in human society, guiding and leading mankind to higher aims and a nobler morality. Christ is greater than every one of us, and we are Christians in the measure that his soul has taken its abode in us.

The Christ of the gospels, however, who has become the religious ideal of Christianity, is very different from the Christ of the Christians—or, let us rather say, of those who call themselves Christians, who worship Christ in a truly pagan manner. Those who call themselves after Christ are, upon the whole, the least worthy of the name, for, if he came unto his own, his own would receive him not.

The so-called faithful Christians have made themselves a religion little better than that of fetish worshippers and practice in many respects an ethics exactly opposite to the injunctions of Christ. Their worship consists in adoration and genuflections and other heathenish rituals, but they violate his commands. They believe in the letter of mythological traditions, and fail to recognise the spirit of the truth.

Let us here briefly pass in review some important religious issues which present a strong contrast between Christ and the so-called Christians.

* * *

Christ is the way, the truth, and the life, but those who in public life ostentatiously set themselves up as Christians bar the way, dim the truth, and impede life. They demand a blind belief in confessions of faith and other man-made formulas, while they trample under foot any one who dares to search for the truth or walk in the way of progress.

Christ is the way, which means, the spirit of evolution, of a constant moral perfectionment; but the Christians, in name, have become a clog on the feet of mankind, so that they are known as the chief suppressors of truth, liberty, and progress.

Says Christ :

"Well hath Esaias prophesied of you hypocrites as is written, 'This people honoreth me with their lips, but their heart is far from me.'

"Howbeit in vain do they worship me, teaching for doctrines the commandments of men.

"For laying aside the commandment of God, ye hold the tradition of men !. . . Full well ye reject the commandment of God that ye may keep your own tradition."—Mark, vii.

Which is the will of God : the injunctions preached by preachers and priests, or the everlasting revelation in the book of nature? The former we have to accept on trust ; the latter every one can find out for himself by experience. The former are inconsistent, varying and unreliable; the latter can be investigated and veri-fied. The literatures of all nations, including espe-cially the scriptures of our religious traditions, have been written in order to assist us in deciphering the revelations of God as they appear in the immutable laws of nature. Let us search the scriptures, and let us study the works of our scientists. But always bear in mind that truth is God's revelation, be it pronounced by Isaiah or Darwin, and not this or that formula, or holy writ, or sacred tradition, and, least of all, a *qui-cunque.*

When certain of the Pharisees said to the disciples of Jesus : "Why do ye that which is not lawful to do on the Sabbath days?" Jesus, answering them, said :

"What man shall there be among you, that shall have one sheep, and if it fall into a pit on the Sabbath day, will he not lay hold on it and lift it out?

"How much then is a man better than a sheep? Wherefore it is lawful to do well on the Sabbath days. . . .

"The Sabbath was made for man, and not man for the Sab-bath :

"Therefore the Son of man is Lord also of the Sabbath."

The Christians of the first century abolished the Sabbath and introduced Sunday as a sacred day; and their Sunday was not a day of rest, but a remembrance of Christ's resurrection.   The Christians of our time, however, know not how to celebrate the day. Although they believe literally in the resurrection, Christ has not risen in their souls.

The name-Christians revive the old pagan notion that the Sunday is to be regarded as a *dies ater*, an ominous day, on which it is not advisable to undertake anything.   They make of man the slave of Sunday; they close places of harmless pleasures and useful information, and in such efforts they find a strong support by men of evil enterprises, who offer to the people more exciting and less innocent amusements.   Must Christ come again to repeat the question:

"Is it lawful on the Sabbath days to do good or to do evil? to save life or to destroy life?"

Is there any one who doubts that museums, good theatres,* and libraries furnish recreations which exercise a strong influence for good upon the development of man's mind?   They provide a wholesome mental food, educating without the toil of study and broadening our views.   They are not idle pleasures; they are building up and life-saving; they are, if enjoyed in the right spirit, truly religious, and Christ teaches that it is right to heal, to help, and to save on the Sabbath.

Some of the early Christians continued to celebrate the Sabbath after the Jewish fashion, and the apostle St. Paul suffered them to do so; yet he insisted vigor-

---

* I say "*good* theatres" on purpose, thinking that vulgar show-pieces might be avoided on Sundays as well as on week-days. But a drama, like Schiller's "Maria Stuart," is a sermon better than any divine can preach.

ously upon liberty in such matters. We read in the epistle to the Romans :

"One man esteemeth one day above another : another esteemeth every day alike. Let every man be fully persuaded in his own mind.

" He that regardeth the day, regardeth it unto the Lord ; and he that regardeth not the day, to the Lord he doth not regard it."

In his letter to the Galatians, however, who piously abstained from the desecration of the Sabbath, the apostle writes :

" Ye observe days, and months, and times, and years.

" I am afraid of you, lest I have bestowed upon you labor in vain."

A wrong conception of the Sabbath is an indication of paganism ; and wherever paganism prevails the spirit of true Christianity bestows its labors in vain.

Woe to ye hypocrites, who make religion ridiculous! Woe to ye Sabbatarians, who make of Christianity a nuisance! Ye are blind leaders of the blind, a disgrace to the holy name which you write upon your altars.

We do not mean to abolish Sunday, or to deprive the laborer of his rest on the seventh day. On the contrary, we insist on keeping Sunday as a religious and also as a secular holiday. But we object to a wrong usage of Sunday, as if it were the Sabbath of the Pharisees. We protest against the barbaric regulations belonging to pre-Christian ages which have been given up by all Christian nations with the sole exception of the English, who, in the beginning of the

middle ages dug them out of the misunderstood religious traditions of a remote past.

We want a Sunday, but not such a Pharisaic Sabbath as is foisted upon the nation by modern Pharisees.   We want a day of rest, of recreation, of edifica-
tion, and not that superstitious *far niente*, which means
a cessation of all wholesome activity.   We want a lib-
eral, a religious, a spiritual, and truly Christian Sunday.

*   *   *

Christ never requested his disciples to eradicate
reason, or to believe anything irrational, or to accept
any of his doctrines in blind trust.   On the contrary,
he wanted them to examine things, to discriminate
between the false and the true, and to discern the
signs of the times.   Our senses should be open to investigation, and our judgment ought to be sound in
order to comprehend things.   He that hath ears to
hear, let him hear, and he who has thoughts to think,
let him think.

How different are Christians !   Christians demand
blind belief ; they do not want investigation ; they
have a distrust of sense information and place no re-
liance upon reason.

What in the world shall we rely on, if reason ceases
to be trustworthy?   If the light of reason be extin-
guished, all our sentiments, our enthusiasm, our aspirations, avail nothing, for without reason, we grope in
the dark.   Says Kant :

"Friends of mankind and of all that is holy to man, accept whatever, after a careful and honest inquiry, you regard to be most trustworthy, be it facts or rational arguments, but do not contest that prerogative of reason, which makes it the highest good upon earth, viz., to be the ultimate criterion of truth. Otherwise you will be unworthy of your liberty and lose it without fail." (Kant, "Was heisst: Sich im Denken orientiren." Edition Hartenstein, Vol. IV, p. 352.)

* * *

Christ abolished prayer in the sense of begging God to do our will, for he truly knew that God, unlike man, is immutable, and his will cannot be altered by supplications.

Christ makes no supplications, no praise, no glorifications of God; he demands no genuflection or self-humiliation. He does not beg for miracles or exceptions or special favors, and in the most wretched moment of his life he remains faithful to this spirit, which lives in his prayer, saying: "Not my, but Thy will be done."

Christ said in the Sermon on the Mount:

"When ye pray, use not vain repetitions. as the heathen do; for they think they shall be heard for their much speaking.

"Be not ye therefore like unto them: for your Father knoweth what things ye have need of, before ye ask him.

"After this manner therefore pray ye: Our Father which art in heaven, hallowed be thy name.

"Thy kingdom come, Thy will be done in earth, as it is in heaven.

"Give us this day our daily bread.

"And forgive us our debts, as we forgive our debtors.

" And lead us not into temptation, but deliver us from evil.*

" For if ye forgive men their trespasses, your heavenly Father will also forgive you :

" But if ye forgive not men their trespasses, neither will your Father forgive your trespasses."

There is but one prayer for our bodily needs—not for our comforts, merely for the needs which, as we must not forget, nature supplies out of her wealth only when we work for them.　There is no prayer for the fulfilment of our particular desires, and all the other requests are variations of the third prayer, which says, " Thy will be done."

The name-Christians actually do use "vain repetitions," so that prayer has almost ceased to have the sense in which Christ used the word.

While recognising the error that obtains in the Christian's habit of praying, we do not mean to discourage the Christian when he wants to pray, for prayer is the moving of the spirit of Christ in the souls of those who know not what Christ is.　If their prayer be honest, it will help them, it will mature them, it will calm their anxieties and make them composed, it will strengthen them, it will make them grow and develop out of their paganism into the Christianity of Christ.　The more they grow in their spiritual life, the more will they cease to prattle to God in childish talk ; they will learn to pray like Christ, until their whole being becomes a performance of God's will.

*The words, " For thine is the kingdom, and the power, and the glory, forever.　Amen," are a later addition.

Any sincere Christian who proposes to himself the question, What shall I pray? in order to pray in the spirit of the Lord's prayer, will come to the conclusion that to ask for special favors is childish as well as useless.

Prayer must be made not with a view of altering God's will, but our own will. We grant, however, that in a certain sense it is true after all that prayer has an influence upon God. Prayer affects our attitude toward God, toward the world, toward our fellow-men, and in so far as our attitude is altered, the attitude of our surroundings will be altered, too. Whether we are impatient and afraid, or calm and self-possessed, makes a great difference, and the whole situation in which we are may change when we pass from one condition into the other. The facts which we face, the dangers which we confront, the duties which we have to perform, assume another countenance; and this change may and very frequently will be the most decisive factor in the final result of our actions.

Take, for instance, our knowledge of nature. The laws of nature have remained the same; but while the savage trembles before the forces of nature, we utilise them to our advantage. The same electricity which was so formidable to our ancestors is to us beneficent. Truly, there is no change in the laws of nature, but a change in our own attitude changes the situation in such a way that it amounts to a most radical change of nature itself.

If knowledge can bring about such wonderful changes, should not the good-will of a religious attitude have the power to reform, to bless, and to save?

*   *   *

Should prayer mean supplication, it would be better that all prayer ceased. And, indeed, the Lord's prayer contains the injunction that we must cease to ask God to do our will.

While Christ's prayer is an act of self-discipline which attunes our will to the will of God, the Christian's prayer is, as a rule, a beggar's supplication, which tries to work miracles. The Christian's prayer may be more refined, but it is actually of the same nature as the medicine-man's incantation, which is supposed to take effect by some mysterious telepathy.

The great Königsberger philosopher uses the word "prayer," not in Christ's sense, but in the sense in which it is used by the name-Christians. He says:

"To expect of prayer other than natural effects is foolish and needs no explicit refutation. We can only ask, Is not prayer to be retained for the sake of its natural effects? Among the natural effects we count that the dark and confused ideas present in the soul are either clarified through prayer, or that they receive a higher degree of intensity; that the motives of virtue receive a greater efficacy, etc., etc.

"We have to say that prayer can, for the reasons adduced, be recommended only subjectively, for he who can in another way attain to the effects for which prayer is recommended will not be in need of it.

"A man may think, 'If I pray to God it can hurt me in no

wise; for should he not exist, very well ! in that case I have done
too much of a good thing ; but if he does exist, it will help me.' This
Prosopopöia (face-making) is hypocrisy, for we have to presuppose
in prayer that he who prays is firmly convinced that God exists.

"The consequence of this is that he who has made great
moral progress ceases to pray, for honesty is one of his principal
maxims. And further, that those whom one surprises in prayer
are ashamed of themselves.

"In public sermons before the public, prayer must be retained, because it can be rhetorically of great effect, and can make
a great impression. Moreover, in sermons before the people one
has to appeal to their sensuality and must, as much as possible,
stoop down to them."

It is especially noteworthy that Kant says "he who
has made great moral progress ceases to pray"; and
he adds the curious observation "that those whom one
surprises in prayer are ashamed of themselves."

The Lord's prayer is no prayer in the common sense
of the word. It is not an incantation that exercises
a supernatural influence through "vain repetitions."
The Lord's prayer must be lived, rather than spoken.
We need not pray it, if we but live it. Its spirit must become part of our soul, so that our whole life becomes an
exemplification of the sentiment, "Thy will be done."

"Further, psychology teaches that very often the exposition
of an idea, weakens the efficacy it possessed, while still whole and
entire, although dark and undeveloped.

"And, finally, there is hypocrisy in prayer ; for the man who
either prays audibly, or who resolves his ideas internally in words,
regards the Deity as something that can be grasped by the senses,
while it is only a principle which his reason urges him to assume.

While Christ's prayer means resignation to the will
of God, the Christian's prayer is a superstitious trust in
miracles, in the hope that they will be performed for
his advantage. Christ's prayer is an effort to change
our own will, not God's will; it is a self-exhortation
which helps us to be satisfied with God's will and to
perform our duties.

These are striking differences between Christ and
Christians, between Christ's faith and the Christian's
faith, between Christ's prayer and the Christian's
prayer, between Christ's religion and ecclesiasticism.
Christ is a savior, a liberator, a reformer; the typical
Christian is a stumbling-block, and a cause of an-
noyance.

There is a wonderful saving power in the words of
Christ, but the name-Christians do not know it. They
walk in darkness and are not even aware of it themselves. They believe themselves to be saints, and are
in fact the spiritual successors of the scribes and
Pharisees.

If ever the name of Christ be dimmed in its glory,
it will be done by the vices of his followers in name,
and the freethinker will have to be called upon to re-
store the lost halo of the greatest reformer and the
staunchest defender of free thought and liberty.

The religion of science is not and cannot be the
Christianity of those who call themselves orthodox
Christians, but it is and will remain the Christianity of
Christ.

THE CATHOLICITY OF THE RELIGIOUS
SPIRIT

THE CATHOLICITY OF THE RELIGIOUS SPIRIT.

The old traditional religions take, as it were, a bee-line in advancing man to the benefits and blessings of truth. They make it possible for man to feel the truth without knowing it; the truth is given him in a mixture with mythology, so that even minds incapable of scientific inquiry can possess and apply it in practical life.

Religion will naturally appear to neophytes who have not entered into its sanctissimum and have never had a glimpse of its esoteric spirit as a mystery; and to those, who, blind to its truth, see its mythology only as a medley of human fraud and folly.

In the assurance of devout piety there is a wisdom that is not discarded by the religion of science. We can have, and we should have, a resolute confidence in the unbreakable and unbroken laws of existence. We can have, and we should have, an intimate and truly personal relation to that All-being in which, through which, and to which we live. This All-being in its wonderful harmony of law surrounds and pervades our entire existence. We cannot withdraw ourselves from its influence, and, truly, it is grand and sublime and perfect beyond description. It is the source of all blessings, and it encompasses us with a beneficence that can be compared only to a father's love. It is greater than a father's love; and is greater than any particular thing we know of, for it comprises all things, and a father's love is only one brilliant ray of its sunshine.

When we regard our own being as a revelation of the All-being, so that our very self is felt to be an in-carnation of nature's divinity, and that our will is identified with God's will, we shall learn to look upon the troubles and anxieties of life with quietude. A heavenly rest will overspread all our being. Whether we struggle and conquer or stumble and fall, whether we are in joy or in sorrow, whether we live or die, we know that it is a greater one than ourselves who suf-fers and struggles and has his being in us and in our aspirations, and his greatness sanctifies the yearnings of our heart and consecrates even the trivialities of life.

We do not exist for enjoyment, for truly pure en-joyment is an impossibility. We live to perform work. We have a mission. There are duties imposed upon us.

And we can gain satisfaction only by performing our work, by complying with our mission, by attend-ing to our duties.

There is no genuine happiness, unless it be the rapture of the God moving in us.

When we consider the letter in which truth is expressed, we find an unfathomable abyss between the religion of science and the dogmatic religions of the established churches. It is the abyss that separates mythology from truth, paganism from sound science, idolatry from self-reliance, superstition from religion, bigotry from righteousness.

When we consider the spirit in which the truth is felt, we find that the spirit is the same in the old historical religions as in the religion of science.

The spirit of almost all the words of the great teachers of mankind is the same as that which must animate the religion of science, and the most beautiful, the profoundest, and sublimest of all sayings are those spoken by the great Master of Galilee.

The spirit of religion is true and noble, but dogmatism affects, like a deadly poison, the religions of mankind. How many of the keenest and most scientific thinkers have been, and are still, through its influence, estranged from the church! Dogmatism warps the sentiments of men and takes away the natural charm that surrounds the holiest enthusiasm. Nevertheless, even in orthodox churchmen the light of true religion sometimes shines undimmed.

One of the founders of Christian dogmatism is St. Augustine. But he is not so narrow as are his followers. Although he sometimes appears narrow, his conception of Christianity is broad, so that he might call it the cosmic religion, the religion of truth, or that re-

ligion which the scientist will find to be founded in the
constitution of the universe. Christianity is to him only
a name which was recently given to the cosmic religion
of universal truth.   He says :

"The very same thing which now is called Christianity existed among the ancients and was not absent in the beginning of
mankind until Christ himself appeared in the flesh, whence the
true religion, which already existed, began *to be called* Christian."
(Retr. I, 13.)*

We are, furthermore, strangely impressed with the
remarkable agreement that obtains, not in the letter,
but in the spirit, between the teachings of the religion
of science and those of Johannes Tauler.

The quotation of a few short passages will suffice
to set this agreement in a clear light.

The chapter which is to be considered as the quintessence of all his preaching, "containing the doctrines
of Tauler in three points, discusses the subject, "how
we shall perfectly go out of ourselves and enter God."

It must be observed that Tauler's terminology is
different from ours.   While "nature," in the terminology of science, is identical with reality, including
all that exists, also the laws of nature and the reality
of our spiritual being, it means to Tauler only the
lower desires of man and that which is apt to elicit
them.   "Nature" means to Tauler what "Sansara"
means to the Buddhist.   It is the sham of our indi-

* *Ipse res quæ nunc Christiana religio nuncupatur, erat apud antiquos nec*
defuit ab initio generis humani, quousque ipse Christus veniret in carne, unde
vera religio quæ jam erat, cæpit appellari Christiana.

vidual existence, the delusion of egotism, and the Vanity Fair of our transient pleasures.

Says Tauler* :

"We now propose three points which contain briefly all that on which we have expatiated in this book.

"The first point is this : He who wants to make progress in his sanctification, to become a real and affirmed friend of God, to love God with all his heart, with all his soul, and with all his mind, and his neighbor as himself, and to truly feel God's presence in his interior, in his heart, all earthly love of and inclination toward anything that is not God must be slain and must remain dead."

We have to remark that there may be a difference of opinion as to what God is and what God is not. For instance, the duties of family life, energetic enterprise in business, admiration of art may have appeared, if not to Tauler, but to any average clergyman of Tauler's time, as ungodly. The religion of science finds God in all things. The religion of science has overcome the error of negativism and has freed us from the shackels of asceticism. But this difference of view as to the nature of God should not prevent us from seeing the concurrence in principles.

Tauler continues :

"The second point demands that if we wish here in time, and there in eternity, to attain to the cognition of the highest truth, we must in all things rid ourselves of all pleasures of the spirit, in which the spirit seeks and means itself. It is so common, alas !

---

* *Medulla Animæ*, Chap. XXVI in Surius's Latin edition, Chap. XXV in the German edition, Chap. XXXIX in Cassender's modern translation. The quotations above are translated from the Cassender edition (Prague, 1872, 2d ed., F. Tempsky).

that having abandoned all the externalities of life, the pleasure of the spirit in us begins to awake. The spirit is pleased with certain fancies and certain ways which it loves as its *alter ego*, which it seeks and aims at; and thus the spirit is captivated in these things and shut out from the true light so that the latter cannot give any enlightenment. The self-loving lust of the spirit to which the spirit loves to surrender itself hinders and dims the rays of divine truth. The exercises, whatever they may be, contemplation, thought, activity, intuition, etc., are not used as means for a pure seeking God, willing God, and meaning God. The spirit rather seeks in them its own self. Their purpose is the ego and not God."

Is this passage not true of all those arguments which are brought forth in favor of an individual immortality of the ego? How often is it claimed that any other immortality but the ego-immortality is unsatisfactory. Truly, the immortality of the soul as taught by science must be unsatisfactory to every one whose religion has not as yet reached the height and purity of Tauler's doctrines. Those who find satisfaction only if they have an ego-immortality, do not seek God in religion, but themselves.

Tauler's second point finds further explanation :

"In this state (of seeking God, willing God, and meaning God) nature must slaughter and sacrifice its pleasure ; its seeking self must die entirely. . . . This means in the proper sense of the word, to die off to one's self. It is a real *entwerden* (a becoming nothing), an annihilation, a losing, a resignation. Nothing remains but God ; nothing is retained but He ; there is no rest but in Him ; so that God, in and with man, can do His will, so that God alone be willing, working, illumining, and moving in man, man being nothing of his own accord, neither willing, nor working, nor illumining, nay, even not existing except as that which God is in him ; so that man is nothing at all in his ways, works, and objects ; i. e , in all things man should seek himself neither in time nor in eternity."

"The third point of the whole doctrine is this : When man has freed himself externally and internally of any and all pretensions, when he has reached the state, in the way we have indicated, of standing upon his nothingness, then alone can he freely enter into the highest and simplest good—into God. His entrance however, must be thorough and not in part. . . . O, what bliss lies in such moments ! . . . . One such entrance into God is sublimer and more excellent than many other and often so-called great exercises and works outside of it. In it alone is real divine life and true peace."

Tauler took Christianity seriously and extracted its quintessence. Let us take Tauler seriously, and we come to an agreement with Christianity.

Cling to the meaning of your mythology, O ye faithful ; and you will naturally walk on the right path!

There is this constant objection made, "If the religious doctrines are not literally true, if God is not truly a person, if my ego is a mere illusion, if heaven and hell are conditions of our being and not places somewhere in space, what do I care for the meaning of these parables?"

We answer : The substance is better than the allegory, the meaning is deeper than the mythology, truth is greater than fiction.

He who does not see that the substance is better than the allegory, the meaning deeper than the mythology, and truth greater than fiction, had better cling to the allegory, mythology, and fiction, lest he lose the substance, the meaning, and the truth. His mind is not as yet sufficiently matured to receive the truth.

We cannot feed the babes with meat, we must give them milk.

*   *   *

The main secret of the innumerable blessings and benefits which can be derived from religion lies in this : that by learning how to live we learn to understand the meaning of the world. The mystery of being is revealed only to the man who actually lives a moral life.

Religion on the one hand demands a surrender of all egotistic desires, it teaches us the right spirit in which we must regulate our conduct ; and on the other hand religion gradually accustoms us to viewing life from the higher standpoint of the divinity of nature. We see that which is transient as transient and identify our being with that which is eternal. And the air we breathe on the heights to which religion raises us is bracing, refreshing, and healthy.

The religion of science is not a substitute for the dogmatic and mythological religions of our churches. On the contrary, the church-religions are a substitute for the religion of science ; they are a mere temporary expedient proposing mythologies so long as the truth is not as yet forthcoming. When that which is perfect is come, then that which is in part shall be done away. The mythology is of a passing value but the truth will abide.

IN REPLY TO A FREETHINKER

IN REPLY TO A FREETHINKER.

The Religion of Science has been severely criticised in a series of articles that appeared in the *Freethought Magazine* and were afterwards republished in pamphlet-form under the title *"Religion and Science,* the Reconciliation Mania of Dr. Paul Carus of *The Open Court* Analysed and Refuted by Corvinus."

Identifying the negativism of his peculiar free-thought with Science, and Religion with superstition, Corvinus denounces every attempt at reconciliation between Religion and Science, and condemns my expositions of a religion that would be in accord with Science as a "conglomeration of self-contradictory ideas," which display "inconsistency" and "ambiguity." He calls me a "freethinker in disguise," and contrasts such passages in which I appear as "virtually a freethinker" with others in which I maintain the existence of God and the immortality of the soul.

There are plenty of misrepresentations in Corvinus's criticism, but they are apparently involuntary. It is true that I use many old words, such as Religion, God, soul, and immortality, in a new sense, but I have always been careful to explain what I mean. Had I ever tried to dodge the truth, or leave people in doubt as to my opinions, there would be some justice in the accusations of Corvinus. The fact is that my definitions are new mainly because they are more definite than those handed down to us by tradition.

My method of reconciliation consists in showing the dogmatic believer a way out of his narrowness. I undertake to instruct him in the meaning of his religion, pointing out how he can decipher the symbols of his creed and transfigure them into exact truth. At the same time I give to the freethinker the key which will unlock the mysteries of traditional religion, and exhibit the significance of their peculiar forms, so full of beauty and comfort to the believer, and so grotesque to the uninitiated.

That Corvinus judges rashly of the work which I do, is, in my opinion, simply due to the fact that he never felt the need of a reconciliation of religion with science, and science with religion. He knows neither the real character of the religious people of to-day, nor does he understand the historical import of religion. He only knows the little circle of his own society, in which freethought prevails, and he has probably never investigated the evolution of moral ideals, which, without religion, would never have been disseminated or enthusiastically received among the masses of mankind. Morality without religion, and of course we mean here religion in the highest sense of the word, would have simply been fear of the police, and nothing more.

Corvinus has misunderstood the most important side of my position. He sees the negations alone of my philosophy, which ally me so strongly with the freethinker party, but not its affirmations, and I would say, that if to be a freethinker means to be purely negative and to reject wholesale everything that has been established by the millennial evolution of religion, I am not a freethinker, but I am an orthodox among the orthodox ; nay, an arch-orthodox, for while the old-fashioned orthodoxy claims to be a system of belief, the new orthodoxy which is implied in the Religion of Science claims to be based on a firmer foundation than mere belief.* It is built upon evidence which can be rejected only by those who are unable to comprehend the import of facts.

To Corvinus, all religions, and especially Christianity, are errors and unmitigated nonsense, while I see in them the development of that most important side of man's nature, which determines the character of his life. In my opinion, the very idea of "a system of pure ethics" is unscientific. Ethics is always the expression of a world-conception. Every religion and every philosophy has its own ethics. Cut ethics loose from its basis, and it remains an arbitrary system of rules without either *raison d'être* or authority. The

---

* See the author's article, "The New Orthodoxy," a paper read before the Pan-American Congress of Religion and Education, Toronto, 1895 ; published in *The Monist*, Vol. VI., No. 1, pp. 91–98.

raison d'être of moral commandments is the most essential part of ethics ; it is the root from which morality springs, and whatever this *raison d'être* be, it is the
religion of the man who owns it.   If there are men
who have no other *raison d'être* for moral conduct than
their own personal welfare, I would say that their religion consists in the attainment of happiness. If they
recognise no authority to which they bow save their
own pleasure or displeasure, their God is Self.   Now,
it has been maintained by some freethinkers that the
very nature of freethought consists in this unshackled
freedom, and I would say that if their conception is
truly legitimate freethought, I am no freethinker, for I
believe, nay, I know, that there is a power in this world
which we have to recognise as the norm of truth and
the standard of right conduct ; and, indeed, there are
conditions in which our personal happiness may seriously come into conflict with our duties.   In this sense
I uphold the idea of God as being a supreme authority
for moral conduct, the presence of which in life can
only be denied by men whose opposition to the false
dogmatism of the traditional religions leads them to
deny also their truth, which is their very essence, and
the cause of their continued existence.

Religion, as it originates among the various nations
of the world, is not the product of systematised investigation, but of race-experience.   It is natural that
truths of great importance were, long before a scientific investigation could explain their nature, invented

by instinct. Thus the Egyptians invented imple-
ments, the use of which is based on laws utterly un-
intelligible in those days. In the same way moral
truths were proclaimed by the prophets, who felt their
significance without being able to explain them by a
philosophical argumentation, and it is to the enormous
practical importance of these truths that they owe
their survival. To show justice and mercy to enemies
appears at first sight foolish, but experience has taught
that the men who insisted on this principle were right,
and the belief in their divine mission became by and
by established. The prophets of almost all nations
were persecuted, but their doctrines survived, and led
naturally enough to the foundation of institutions such
as the synagogue of the Jews, the church of the Christians, the sangha of the Buddhists.

The religious conception which it is my life-work
to uphold, is simple enough, yet I find that Corvinus
has radically misunderstood its main significance,
without which all my writing would indeed be a mere
quibbling of words and an ambiguous display of old
phrases, not in a new sense, but without any sense.

One instance will be sufficient to point out the misconception of Corvinus. Corvinus declares that God
is with me ''only an idea," implying that it is no reality. He says (p. 31):

"If God is being defined simply as abstract thought, an idea,
as something *existing only in imagination and not in reality*, it is
meaningless to say, 'Science is a revelation of God.'"

And he adds:

"Science is the achievement of man and nothing else."

In opposition to his statement I say that the idea of God is an abstract thought, but God himself is a reality. There is no abstract thought but it is in-vented to describe a reality.* If the term "God" did not describe an actual reality, it would be meaningless to speak of "Science as a revelation of God." I grant that Science is "the achievement of man," but that is one side only of the truth. Far from being "the achievement of man *and nothing else*," Science is in its very essence superhuman. Man cannot invent math-ematics; he must discover its theorems. He cannot make the laws of nature; he must describe them. He cannot establish facts; he must investigate, and can only determine the truth. Nor can he set up a code of morals, but he must adapt himself to the eternal moral law which is the condition of human society and the factor that shapes the human of man.

Here is the point where Corvinus radically differs from my position. He says, quoting a misunderstood passage from Haeckel:

"'Constantly to speak of the moral laws of nature proves blindness to the undeniable facts of human and natural history.'"

Corvinus adds:

"All moral laws from their beginning in the dim past among

* An apparent exception to this rule is the conception of the irrational in mathematics. The irrational is a symbol representing a function which can-not be performed. The root-extraction of (—1) is as impossible as the squar-ing of the circle.

our rude, savage-like predecessors up to the noblest conceptions of modern ethics, were conceived, proposed, and consequently established by man."

Corvinus says that "necessity gave birth to these moral laws," meaning probably by necessity "the needs of man." I accept his reply, and would say that the needs of man indicate the presence of a higher necessity, viz., of that necessity which we trace in the harmony of natural laws and in the peculiarly complicated simplicity of mathematics. This higher neces-sity is the ultimate *raison d'être* of the moral law, and it is a characteristic feature of that omnipotent presence which we can trace everywhere. Intrinsic necessity means eternality, immutability, stern and inflexible authority—in a word, it means God.

Corvinus confounds two things : moral injunctions and the natural law of morality. Moral injunctions are proposed and established by man in his anxiety to adapt himself to the moral law, exactly as an architect may write down the rules for building bridges so that according to the material which he uses the law of gravitation shall not be infringed upon. If the architect's rules are in conformity with the natural conditions, such as scientists formulate in what is called laws of nature, he will be able to build boldly and securely. And if the laws of legislators are based upon a correct conception of the moral law of nature, the nations who adopt them will prosper and progress.

It appears that, according to Corvinus, the moral

law of nature is a nonentity, while the injunctions of
law-givers are all that can be called a moral law. The
fact is just the reverse. The moral law of nature is
the eternal abiding reality, while the laws and injunctions of man are only its transitory and more or less
imperfect expressions. The moral law of nature alone
partakes of that feature which in all religions is attrib-
uted to God. It is eternal, it is omnipresent, it is irrefragable. Certainly the moral law is not a concrete
object, not an individual fact, not a personal being,
but for that reason it is not a nonentity. It cannot be
seen with the eye, or heard with the ear, or tasted with
the tongue, or touched with the hands. It is one of
those higher realities which can only be perceived by
the mind. The senses are insufficient to encompass
it, but any normal mind can grasp it.

There was in the Middle Ages a philosophical party
called the Nominalists, who denied the objective existence of ideas, declaring ideas to be mere names
without any corresponding reality. Their adversaries,
called the Realists, believed in the reality of ideas.
And while the nominalistic philosophy was rejected,
it began to flourish again and found its mightiest expression in the transcendental idealism of the great
sage of Königsberg. On this line of thought the whole
universe becomes intrinsically incomprehensible, end-
ing at last in agnosticism, in which Nominalism reaches
its final *reductio ad absurdum.*

Corvinus is apparently a nominalist. Ideas are to

him mere ideas, i. e., subjective inventions without objective reality ; and science, that most methodical system of ideas, is not a revelation of objective truth, but "the achievement of man and nothing else." It is, accordingly, in the same predicament as the names of the nominalists, and he who studies science is like Hamlet in one of his erratic moods reading, as he says, "Words, words, words." Science would be mere words without any objective significance.

Now I will not quarrel with Corvinus about names. He has an inherited objection to the very word "God." I will not now apply the name God to that peculiar presence of superhuman reality which the various sciences reveal to us in parts, but I insist on its being a reality; indeed, I maintain that it is the most real reality in the world. We may call it cosmic order, or law (*Gesetzmässigkeit*), or necessity, or the eternal, or the immutable, or the omnipresent, the absolute, or the prototype of mind, or the standard of rationality, or the universal Logos, or the authority of conduct. But it exists, in undeniable objectivity. We cannot mould it or shape it, but, on the contrary, we are the products of its handiwork. Every arithmetical formula, every law of nature, every truth, is a partial revelation of its character, and there is nothing in the infinite universe but is swayed by its influence. It encompasses the motions of the infinitesimal atoms and of the grandest suns ; it is the logic of man's reason and the nobility of man's moral aspirations.

It is true that I deny the existence of an individual God. In this sense I am an outspoken atheist. Nevertheless, I declare most emphatically that *God is a reality*, and indeed, God is a super-individual reality. In Corvinus's opinion this is a flat contradiction and he has no other explanation of it than by considering it as a tergiversation. He puts it down as a mania through which I try to reconcile the errors of the past with the truths of modern times. By truths of modern times he understands negations of all and any positive issues in religion, so that as soon as I attempt to formulate freethought in positive terms, which is tantamount to recognising the truth in our traditions, he decries me for pandering to popular superstitions.

In my opinion freethought has been barren because of its negativism and it is now behind the times because it has failed to come out with positive issues, and now that The Open Court Publishing Co. is proposing a constructive freethought, its work is suspected, criticised, and rejected by freethinkers. In spite of the negations of Corvinus, I insist that the reality of God is an undeniable fact, scientifically provable by unfailing evidence. It can be established so surely that Corvinus, as soon as he grasps the meaning of the idea, would say that it is a truism.

Philosophical materialism has so strongly affected our ideas that the average mind is incapable of believing in immaterial realities. First, the immaterial realities of natural laws were represented as personal beings, then as metaphysical essences, and now since we know that metaphysicism is untenable their very existence is denied, and, being recognised as immaterial, they are declared to be unreal. But the objective reality of form and the laws of form is exactly the truth which we must learn to appreciate.

That which the senses do not perceive, but is discernible by the mind, is not non-existent but possesses a higher kind of existence. It constitutes the unity of the universe and the harmony of its order. Without it, the world would not be a cosmos but an incoherent chaos ; nature would be matter in motion, without any regularity of mechanical adjustment and the system of thought-forms which constitutes the superiority of the human mind would never have developed. Without it, Science would be mere verbiage, Religion meaningless, and ethics an impossibility.

The new philosophy which I represent—call it Monism, or the New Positivism (for it differs from Comtean Positivism), or the Philosophy of Science, or the New Realism—insists on the reality of form and of relations, and on the significance of ideas. The soul of man is not in his blood but in his mind. He is not a mere heap of atoms. He consists of ideas. His existence is not purely material. It is also, and principally, spiritual. We grant that there is no ego-soul. There is as little a metaphysical thing-in-itself of man as there is a thing-in-itself of a watch, or of a tree, or of a natural law. But nevertheless, just as much as that combination which makes of a spring, cogs and wheels, an instrument called a watch, is not a non-entity but a reality, in the same way man's soul in spite of the non-existence of a metaphysical ego-soul is not a nonentity but a reality; and the mould into which we have been cast is that divinity of the world which was at the beginning and will remain for ever and aye.

If there is anything that deserves the name of God-head, it is this peculiar supersensible Reality, the various aspects of which are revealed in glimpses that we receive in Religion, in Ethics, and in Science. For here alone the attributes of divinity are found, viz., omnipresence and universality, immutability and eternity, intrinsic necessity and irrefragability. It is one and the same in all its various revelations, in mathematical theorems and in ethical injunctions. There is no wisdom, but it is a comprehension of *its* truth. There is no virtue, but it is a compliance with *its* dispensations. There is no genuine piety, but it is a devotion to *its* beauty and sovereignty. If there are gods of any kind, *it* is the God of gods, and if the word supernatural has any sense, here is it applicable; for here we have the conditions for all possible worlds, and it would remain such as it is, even if nature did not exist. The simplest formulas of arithmetic as well as the noblest moral laws, which constitute the superiority of love over hate and of compassion over ferocity, hold good for this actual world of ours not less than for any possible world.

Thus we learn that if God is not wise like a sage, he is infinitely more than wise ; he is that which constitutes the essence of all wisdom. God is not good like a well-meaning man ; he is more than a philanthropist. God is the measure of goodness and the moral law of life.

When Corvinus speaks of God he means the God-conception of average Christianity. But we can assure him that the masses are not responsible for the religion which they espouse, while many leaders in the churches are far from believing in an individual God. They may not be clear as to the nature of God. They believe in Him without comprehending his Being ; but I maintain that upon the whole they have an aspiration toward a higher conception and that in the long run of the historical evolution of mankind they will more and more accept the idea of God as the Religion of Science conceives it now. They try to conceive the idea of God as a truly superpersonal God, and at the same time think of him still as an individual being, a huge world-ego. But I venture to say that this combination is self-contradictory. If such an individual God, a kind of world-ego, a distinct and single being, existed, if this God were a being who had been the creator of the universe and is now its governor and supreme ruler, I would say that that superpersonal Divinity, the revelation which we find in science, and the essence of which is that indescribable presence of law and cosmic order, must be considered superior to him.

Suppose we call an individual God, after the precedent of the gnostics, "Demiurge" or world-architect and represent him, not as the prototype of all personality, but as an actual person like ourselves, only infinitely greater. Now, suppose that it was he who made the world as a watchmaker makes a watch, that he regulates it as we wind and set our watches, and that he owns and rules it, and keeps it in order. Must we not grant at once that the Demiurge, though infinitely greater than man, would not be the supreme Reality? He would have to obey those supernatural laws of nature which constitute their intrinsic necessity. He would not be the ultimate ground of morality and truth. There is a higher authority above him. And this higher and highest authority is the God of the Religion of Science, who alone is worthy of the name of God. The God of the Religion of Science is still the God of the Demiurge. The Demiurge could have created the world only by complying with the eternal and unalterable laws of being to which he would be not less subject than all his creatures.

Taking this ground, we say that the God of the Religion of Science alone is God, and not the Demiurge in whom a great number of the Christians of to-day still believe. The Demiurge is a mythical figure, and belief in him is true paganism. Monotheism in this sense is only a polytheism which has reduced the number of its gods to one single god-being. The God whom the Religion of Science proclaims is not a single God-Being, but it is the one, the sole, the self-consistent, universal sameness of divinity that is the all-pervading condition of any possible world as a cosmic universe.

The God whom the Religion of Science proclaims is not a new God, but it is the old God proclaimed by every genuine prophet, among the Jews and also among the Gentiles, only purified of its paganism.

The Philosophy of Science is not an absolutely new philosophy, but only a more distinct formulation of the principles which have long been practised among scientists. In the same way, the Religion of Science is not a radically new religion, but a religious reform which, according to the needs of the time, matures the old religions and opens a vista into the future, in which the most radical freethought is reconciled with the most rigorous orthodoxy. And this is not done by artificial phrases or by tergiversation, but by fusing religion in the furnace of science, and by sifting our religious traditions in the sieve of critique.

INDEX.

119

INDEX.

INDEX.